Editor
Mary S. Jones, M.A.

Managing Editor
Ina Massler Levin, M.A.

Illustrator
Kelly McMahon

Cover Artist
Tony Carrillo

Art Production Manager
Kevin Barnes

Art Coordinator
Renée Christine Yates

Imaging
Craig Gunnell

Publisher
Mary D. Smith, M.S. Ed.

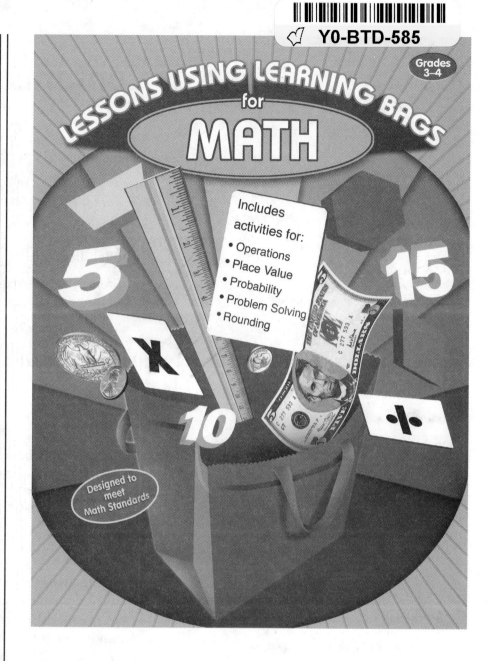

LESSONS USING LEARNING BAGS
for
MATH

Grades 3–4

Includes activities for:
- Operations
- Place Value
- Probability
- Problem Solving
- Rounding

Designed to meet Math Standards

Author

Diane L. Nees

Teacher Created Resources

Teacher Created Resources, Inc.
6421 Industry Way
Westminster, CA 92683
www.teachercreated.com
ISBN-1-4206-3192-6
©2006 Teacher Created Resources, Inc.
Made in U.S.A.

Table of Contents

Introduction

Gift bags are amazing! Their purpose is to contain and transport needed materials. In this case, when used in the classroom, these same bags can contain and transport an incredible number of skills and strategies to students. Gift bags are so colorful, plentiful, easy to use, and inexpensive. What more could a teacher want?

Everywhere you look there are gift bags with designs that fit into any curriculum. Bags come in a multitude of sizes and shapes, which makes coordinating them with lessons, stories, or units a fairly simple task. Make this your goal. Keep a watchful eye out for bag designs that fit your stories or curriculum. In this book, "small" refers to a 7" x 9" bag, "medium" refers to 10" x 12", and "large" refers to 12" x 14". These are approximate sizes and can certainly vary some, depending on the room you have or the bag you find. For many of the activities, the bags are the transport—that is, they will hold all the other materials needed, thereby keeping everything in one spot and readily accessible. All you need to do is copy the "Bag Tag" and use wide, clear tape to attach it to the gift bag as a label for that activity. The color and/or design of each gift bag is up to you. The more colorful and attractive the design of the bags, the more students will inquire about its contents. It is recommended that the bags you choose have sturdy handles.

Bags are versatile and store easily. They can fold flat to fit inside of a file. Bags can also collapse so that you can fit several in a plastic basket to take out and fill as needed. In addition, they can be held on hooks on your bulletin board or around the room. An added bonus is that their designs will add to your classroom décor.

Bags have a great attribute of space . . . unknown space. Students are naturally intrigued by such space and will want to fill that space or find out what's in it. That is the key . . . to motivate! When students are intrigued and motivated—and they will be—you'll open the door to opportunities; active learning experiences; and knowledge of strategies that will promote, challenge, and increase students' understanding. With this understanding, they will learn to become life-long learners.

The activities within these pages meet the McREL math standards, which are listed below. All standards are used with permission from McREL.

- Uses a variety of strategies in the problem-solving process.

- Uses basic and advanced procedures while performing the processes of computation.

- Understands and applies basic and advanced concepts of probability.

Copyright 2004 McREL

Mid-continent Research for Education and Learning

2550 S. Parker Road, Suite 500

Aurora, CO 80014

Telephone: (303) 337-0990

Website: www.mcrel.org/standards-benchmarks

Auction in a Bag

Learn an auctioneer's lingo and gear your students up for an hour of fun and learning! They will learn to count money in a heartbeat, make decisions about costs and risks, and easily be able to tell you what changes they would make if they met up with an auction again!

Materials and Preparation

➤ 1 medium gift bag, labeled Auction in a Bag

➤ 25 envelopes of play money, one for each student with an assortment of money (1 ten, 1 five, 4 ones, 2 half dollars, 4 quarters, 5 dimes, 5 nickels, 5 pennies; use more if you like)

➤ 1 copy of Auction Coupons, page 5. Copy and cut apart for use during the auction.

➤ 10–20 auction items (including the Auction Coupons)

Procedure

1. Hold a simulated auction! You're the auctioneer. Display the auction items on a table and have six students at a time look over the merchandise.

2. After all students have previewed the items, choose one student to hold up the items and one to collect the money during the auction.

3. Give the rest of the students an envelope filled with play money as stated above, with equal money amounts.

4. Have students count their money first and then explain the auction procedure to them. Tell students that they are to raise their hand in order to make a bid on an item, and that they cannot shout out a bid until they have been called on. Optional: If you choose to make auction paddles, have students purchase one for bidding during the auction.

5. The object of this auction is for students to use their money wisely. They need to try to get the most for their money and not be short in the end; without enough money to buy more than one item, or without a purchase.

6. As students purchase items, they should give the exact change to the chosen money collector. If they do not have exact change, they must give more than what is owed, and state the change that they are to get back.

7. Continue the auction until all of the auction items have been purchased.

Bag Tag

4

Auction Coupons

Fifteen minutes of Free Time!

Be a library assistant for 20 minutes!

Read to younger students in another class!

Win one night with NO math homework!

Win one night with NO math homework!

One day of being the teacher's helper!

Sit anywhere you want in the room for one day!

Be the teacher's assistant for one afternoon!

This coupon is good for one free pencil!

This coupon is good to play two games with a friend!

Connectors

Besides computational skills being refreshed, *Connectors* is aimed at making sure students have good number sense. Moving from one given number to the next in order to supply the correct operation takes much reasoning. Don't let the answers slide by without a good explanation of math reasoning.

Materials and Preparation

➤ 1 medium gift bag, labeled Connectors

➤ 5 copies of Connector Clip Labels, page 7. One for each group. Laminate (if possible), copy, and cut apart.

➤ 5 sturdy copies of each: Connector Sheet 1, Connector Sheet 2, and Connector Blank Sheet, pages 8–10. This can be accomplished in a few ways: copy directly onto heavy cardstock, copy on paper then paste to heavy cardstock, or copy and laminate.

➤ 180 small paper clips

Tip: It is recommended that you copy each Connector Sheet and its corresponding labels onto colored paper, making sure each set has a different color.

Procedure

1. Be sure to cut out the Connector Clip Labels for Connector Sheet 1 and Connector Sheet 2 before beginning the lesson. Paperclip each set of labels together or place each set in a separate labeled resealable plastic bag.

2. Have students get into five small groups and work together to complete Connector Sheets 1 and 2. Explain to students that each letter on their sheet represents a math operation (shown on Connector Clip Labels). They should use a paper clip to secure the correct label next to the letter it represents.

3. When finished, have groups share and compare. Read aloud, or write on the board or overhead the Connectors Answer Key (bottom of page) for students to check their answers.

4. Now it's time to have each group make their own Connector Sheet using the blank form on page 10. In addition to writing numbers in the empty spaces, students need to make answer labels with math operations to make it work. (Use blank labels on page 7.)

5. After the groups have finished creating their own sheets, have them switch sheets and labels with each other for more practice in reasoning and computation.

6. Monitor the groups to ensure that the student-created Connector Sheets work.

Connectors Answer Key

Sheet 1	Sheet 2	Bag Tag
A. + 500	A. x 2	
B. x 2	B. ÷ 5	
C. ÷ 5	C. + 4,288	
D. + 1,000	D. − 3,000	
E. ÷ 4	E. ÷ 6	
F. + 70	F. + 690	
G. + 5,000	G. + 2,082	
H. ÷ 2	H. − 1,072	
I. − 2,000	I. ÷ 4	
J. x 5	J. x 5	
K. − 4,060	K. ÷ 2	
L. + 3,800	L. + 30	

Connector Clip Labels

Copy and cut apart. Be sure to keep each set separate.

Labels for Connector Sheet 1

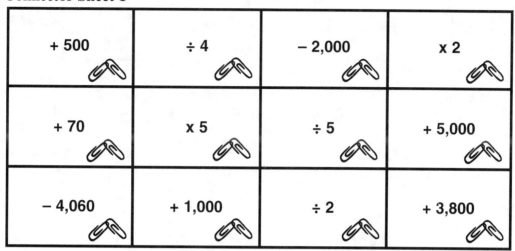

+ 500	÷ 4	− 2,000	x 2
+ 70	x 5	÷ 5	+ 5,000
− 4,060	+ 1,000	÷ 2	+ 3,800

Labels for Connector Sheet 2

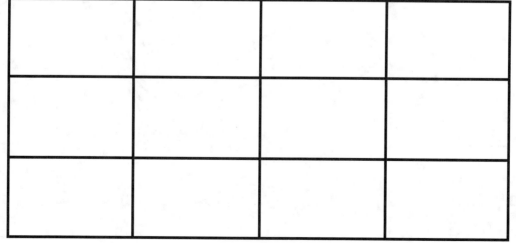

+ 4,288	÷ 6	÷ 4	x 2
+ 690	x 5	÷ 5	− 1,072
÷ 2	− 3,000	+ 2,082	+ 30

Blank Labels for Connector Blank Sheet

Connector Sheet 1

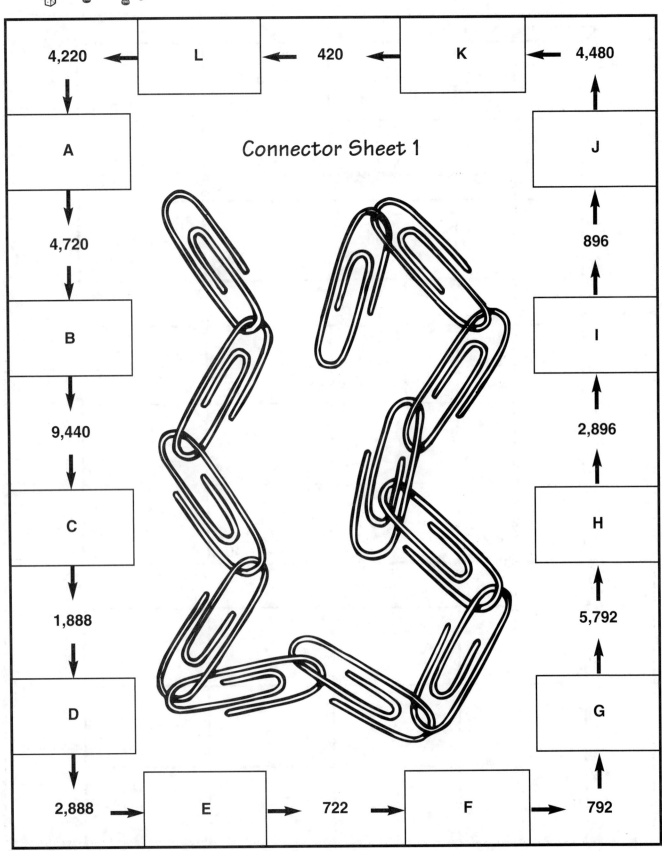

Connector Sheet 1

4,220 ← L ← 420 ← K ← 4,480

A

4,720

B

9,440

C

1,888

D

2,888 → E → 722 → F → 792

J

896

I

2,896

H

5,792

G

Connector Sheet 2

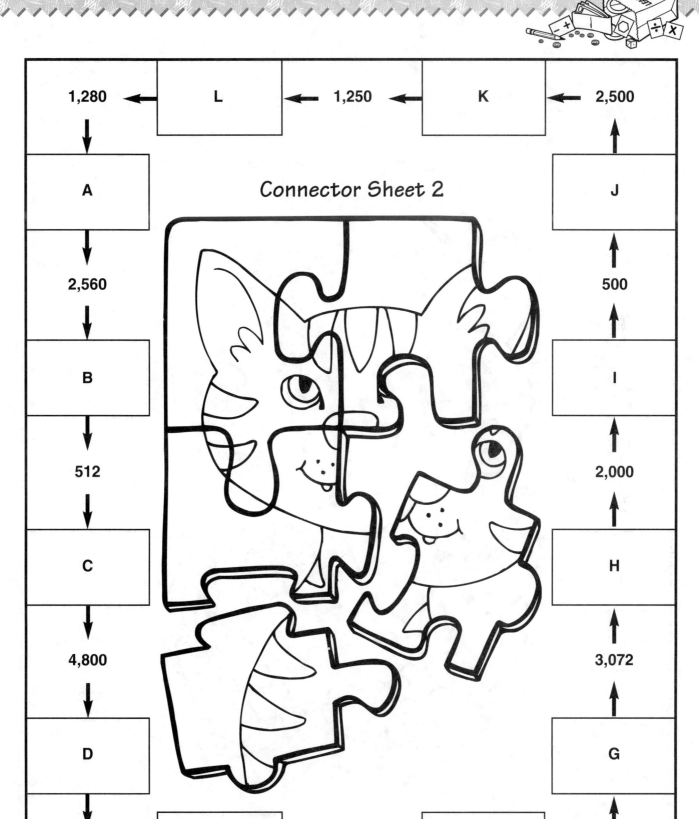

Connector Sheet 2

1,280 ← L ← 1,250 ← K ← 2,500

A

2,560

B

512

C

4,800

D

1,800 → E → 300 → F → 990

J

500

I

2,000

H

3,072

G

Connector Blank Sheet

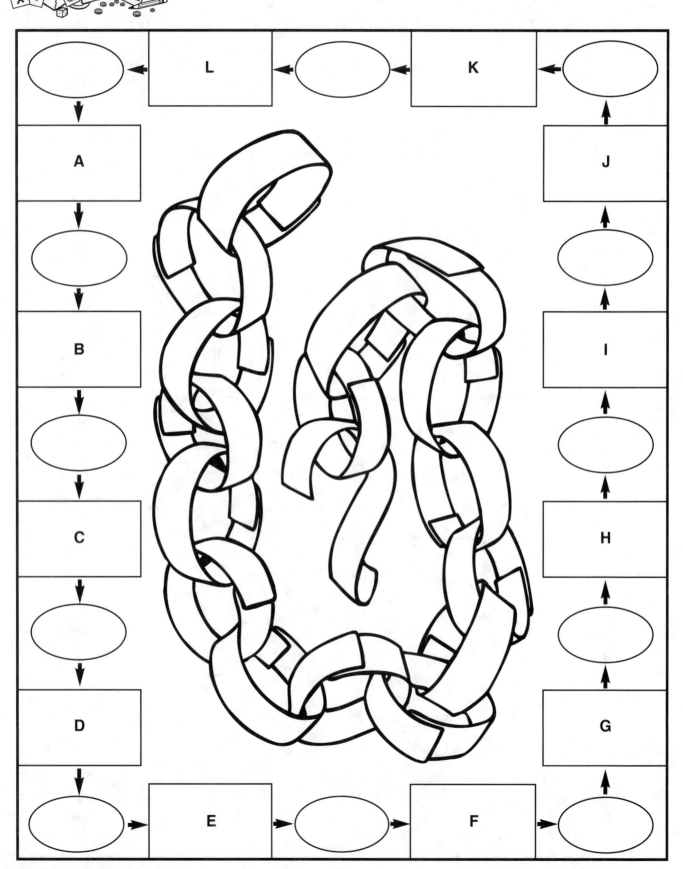

L K

A J

B I

C H

D G

E F

10

Division Bag

Practice, practice, practice . . . that's what it's all about! In this activity, the smaller set of bags will hold the practice sheets, fold forms, and score sheets, while the medium bag will carry the entire set of division practice tool bags.

Materials and Preparation

➤ 1 medium gift bag, labeled Division Bag
➤ 6 small gift bags (Look for ones that will fold flat. Usually a lighter weight bag without any type of laminate will work the best.)
➤ 1 copy of each Division Practice Sheet, pages 12–14. Copy and cut apart. Each will be glued to the front side of a small gift bag. You may need to enlarge these sheets. Laminating each sheet before gluing will make them more durable.
➤ Several copies of the Division Fold Forms, page 15. Copy and cut apart.
➤ Several copies of the Division Practice Score Sheets, page 16. Copy and cut apart.
➤ 12 game pieces, about 1" round, can be flat (stones, checkers, flat wooden pieces, etc.)

Procedure

1. Glue one Division Practice Sheet to the front side of each of the six small gift bags.
2. Put two game pieces, three copies of the Division Fold Forms, and two Division Practice Score Sheets into each bag.
3. While you work with a large group, have 12 students pair up for division practice with the bags. Give each pair of students one bag.
4. They will remove the contents and lay them aside. Have students fold their bag flat, with the Division Practice Sheet side face-up. The first player should toss his or her game piece onto the Division Practice Sheet and say the answer to the fact depending on where it lands. For example, if working on the 2's board (top number is 2 and that's the divisor), and their game piece lands on 16 (representing $16 \div 2 = ?$), they will say 8. Whoever says the answer first scores one point and puts a tally mark by his or her name on the score sheet. The two players will alternate tossing the game pieces and calling out quotients until one player reaches 25 points.
5. Next, they should write all the facts they can think of for their divisor on the Division Fold Forms and use them to practice.

Sample of Division Fold Form: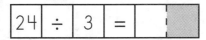

Students should write the dividend in the first box, the divisor in the third box, the quotient in the fifth box, and then fold the dotted flap forward to cover the quotient. These will be used for practicing division facts.

Bag Tag ✂

Division Practice Sheets

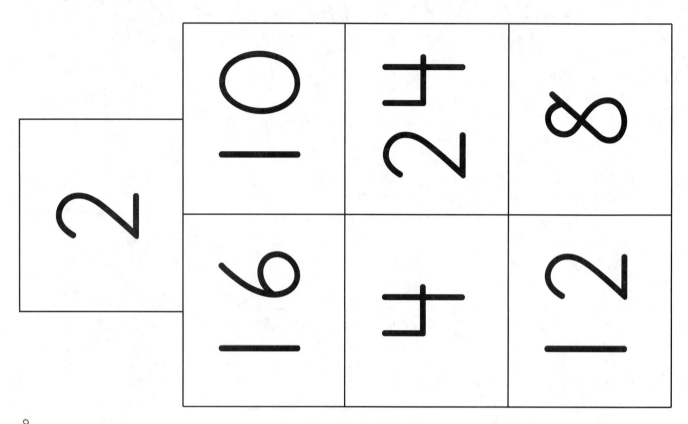

2

10	24	8
16	4	12

✂ -

3

3	24	12
15	6	18

Division Practice Sheets *(cont.)*

4	

32	8	4
16	12	20

✂ -

5	

30	40	15
20	10	45

Division Practice Sheets *(cont.)*

6	12 18	24 30	60 36

7	49 28	14 56	35 21

14

Division Fold Forms

Copy and cut out. Have students write the dividend in the first box, the divisor in the third box, and the quotient in the fifth box. Then they are to fold the dotted flap forward to cover the quotient. These will be used for practicing division facts.

	÷		=		
	÷		=		
	÷		=		
	÷		=		
	÷		=		
	÷		=		
	÷		=		

Division Practice Score Sheets

Division Practice Score Sheet

Give yourself one point for each round you win!

Name _____

Name _____

✂ -

Division Practice Score Sheet

Give yourself one point for each round you win!

Name _____

Name _____

Dollar Exchange

Students can often recite money values, but the real learning comes in their ability to exchange money values—that is, trading five one-dollar bills for a five-dollar bill, two fives for a ten, and so on. This money game bag meets that objective, which leads to understanding.

Materials and Preparation

- ➢ 1 medium gift bag, labeled Dollar Exchange
- ➢ 1 Dollar Exchange Game Board for each student, page 18
- ➢ 1 copy of Money Bills for each student, pages 19–20. Copy, laminate (if possible), cut apart, and place in plastic bags. Optional: Copy onto green paper for a more realistic look.
- ➢ 1 resealable plastic zipper bag for each student, each full of paper money
- ➢ 1 die for each pair of students

Procedure

1. Place students in pairs and distribute one die to each pair and a bag of money and a Dollar Exchange Game Board to each student.

2. Review money combinations. Explain to students that they each have the same items but they will take turns and play against each other (each using a separate game board). The first player to reach the $100.00 wallet with a total of five twenty-dollar bills is the winner.

3. They will do this by taking turns rolling the die to see their dollar amount. For example, if Player 1 rolls a "3," he or she should place three one-dollar bills on the $1.00 wallet. If a "4" is rolled on Player 1's second turn, he or she places four one-dollar bills on the $1.00 wallet and can then exchange five of the seven total dollar bills for a five-dollar bill to place on the $5.00 wallet. (The five one-dollar bills go back in the bag.) Each roll a player makes is to determine the number of one-dollar bills to put down. Players can make exchanges after each roll.

4. You will need to monitor the students to see that exchanges are being made properly. Five one-dollar bills exchange for one five-dollar bill, and that moves a player into the $5.00 wallet. Two five-dollar bills exchange for one ten-dollar bill, and that moves the player into the $10.00 wallet. Two ten-dollar bills exchange for one twenty-dollar bill, and that moves the player into the $20.00 wallet. A collection of five twenty-dollar bills moves a player into the $100.00 wallet and that player wins the game!

Bag Tag

Dollar Exchange Game Board

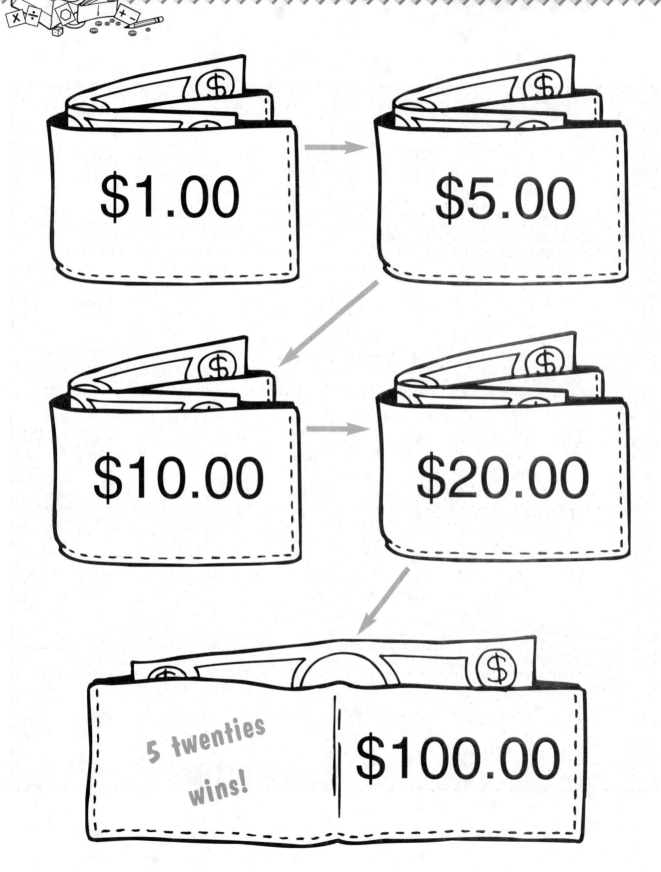

$1.00

$5.00

$10.00

$20.00

5 twenties wins!

$100.00

18

Money Bills

Money Bills *(cont.)*

20

Median, Mode, and Range Bag

Most students need a way to manipulate numbers in order to make the task of learning the concepts of median, mode, and range easier. The list of numbers, or the data set, is not something all students can visualize. The activities in this bag will help students organize and make a visual picture by turning data into meaningful numbers.

Materials and Preparation

➤ 1 medium gift bag, labeled Median, Mode, and Range Bag

➤ 6 copies of Working Mat for each student or group, page 22

➤ 1 copy of each set of Data Picture Cards for each student or group, pages 23–25

➤ scissors for each student or group

➤ glue for each student or group

Procedure

1. This activity should follow a discussion of the terms *median*, *mode*, and *range*. Students may work independently or in small groups.

2. Give each student or group their copies of the Working Mat and the set or sets of Data Picture Cards that you would like them to work on. The cards should be cut out, sorted, and glued onto the Working Mat as if making a bar graph. The numbers should be sorted by column—smallest in the far-left column and highest in the far right column—starting at the bottom of the page.

3. Once sorted, they should interpret the data in terms of what the median, mode, and range of the set are. Have students write down their answers in the boxes provided. Once everyone is finished, share and explain answers as a class or as groups.

4. Allow students time to work with each of the six sets of Data Picture Cards. It is up to you to decide the number of data sets students will work with at one time.

Bag Tag

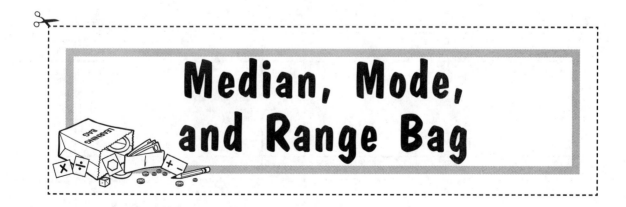

Working Mat

Median—the middle number of a data set when arranged from least to greatest =

Mode—the number that appears most often in a data set =

Range—the difference between the lowest and the highest number in a data set =

<table>
<tr><td></td><td></td><td></td><td></td><td></td><td></td><td></td></tr>
<tr><td></td><td></td><td></td><td></td><td></td><td></td><td></td></tr>
<tr><td></td><td></td><td></td><td></td><td></td><td></td><td></td></tr>
<tr><td></td><td></td><td></td><td></td><td></td><td></td><td></td></tr>
<tr><td></td><td></td><td></td><td></td><td></td><td></td><td></td></tr>
<tr><td></td><td></td><td></td><td></td><td></td><td></td><td></td></tr>
<tr><td></td><td></td><td></td><td></td><td></td><td></td><td></td></tr>
</table>

Data Picture Cards

Cut apart, sort, and glue onto the Working Mat.

Set 1—Dogs

20 lbs.	20 lbs.	27 lbs.	58 lbs.	34 lbs.	51 lbs.
51 lbs.	42 lbs.	58 lbs.	34 lbs.	66 lbs.	51 lbs.
66 lbs.	42 lbs.	58 lbs.	58 lbs.	20 lbs.	51 lbs.
51 lbs.	27 lbs.	34 lbs.	51 lbs.	58 lbs.	20 lbs.

Set 2—Cats

13 lbs.	4 lbs.	4 lbs.	12 lbs.	9 lbs.	9 lbs.
6 lbs.	6 lbs.	7 lbs.	7 lbs.	10 lbs.	9 lbs.
9 lbs.	6 lbs.	10 lbs.	10 lbs.	6 lbs.	7 lbs.
7 lbs.	13 lbs.	9 lbs.	9 lbs.	9 lbs.	4 lbs.

Data Picture Cards *(cont.)*

Cut apart, sort, and glue onto the Working Mat.

Set 3—Children

72 lbs.	48 lbs.	52 lbs.	55 lbs.	68 lbs.	68 lbs.
59 lbs.	60 lbs.	48 lbs.	55 lbs.	68 lbs.	72 lbs.
60 lbs.	68 lbs.	68 lbs.	52 lbs.	52 lbs.	55 lbs.
52 lbs.	59 lbs.	59 lbs.	68 lbs.	60 lbs.	68 lbs.

Set 4—Driving Speeds

52 mph	65 mph	30 mph	36 mph	48 mph	52 mph
52 mph	74 mph	30 mph	60 mph	36 mph	60 mph
36 mph	36 mph	30 mph	30 mph	74 mph	74 mph
60 mph	30 mph	48 mph	36 mph	52 mph	36 mph

24

Data Picture Cards *(cont.)*

Cut apart, sort, and glue onto the Working Mat.

Set 5—Test Scores

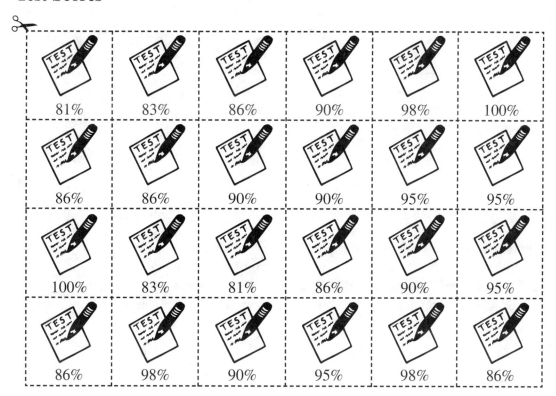

81%	83%	86%	90%	98%	100%
86%	86%	90%	90%	95%	95%
100%	83%	81%	86%	90%	95%
86%	98%	90%	95%	98%	86%

Set 6—Buildings

20 ft.	70 ft.	32 ft.	40 ft.	25 ft.	65 ft.
25 ft.	32 ft.	54 ft.	65 ft.	20 ft.	32 ft.
32 ft.	40 ft.	70 ft.	65 ft.	25 ft.	32 ft.
40 ft.	54 ft.	65 ft.	20 ft.	32 ft.	54 ft.

Multiplication on a Ring

One of the most necessary skills in math is learning basic facts. This bag activity will be full of multiplication facts on rings that will be readily available . . . literally at the students' fingertips!

Materials and Preparation

➤ 1 medium gift bag, labeled Multiplication On a Ring (Use this bag to store the fact rings that students make.)

➤ 1 set of Multiplication Fact Forms for each student, pages 27–31

➤ ½-inch snap key rings to hold Fact Forms together, 1 per student

➤ 1 single hole punch

➤ scissors

Procedure

1. As each set of basic multiplication facts (0–9) is introduced, have students make their own fact form for it; i.e. 0's, 1's, 2's, etc. by writing the answers to the facts in the given boxes. (Note: You may choose to distribute the Multiplication Fact Forms all at once after you have introduced the basic facts for 0–9.) Make sure to copy these single sided so students can cut them apart. Copy onto colored heavy cardstock paper, if available. Optional: After students write their name on the back of each form and correctly fill in all the products, laminate them so that they will be more durable.

2. Ask students to cut out each form leaving the black line around it intact.

3. Use a single hole-punch to make a hole on the top of each form where the black dot is. Distribute the ½-inch snap key rings to students. Add the fact forms to the rings as you teach multiplication.

4. Keep the rings of facts in the labeled gift bag, always ready for student use.

Bag Tag

Multiplication Fact Forms

0 x 0 =

0 x 1 =

0 x 2 =

0 x 3 =

0 x 4 =

0 x 5 =

0 x 6 =

0 x 7 =

0 x 8 =

0 x 9 =

1 x 0 =

1 x 1 =

1 x 2 =

1 x 3 =

1 x 4 =

1 x 5 =

1 x 6 =

1 x 7 =

1 x 8 =

1 x 9 =

Multiplication Fact Forms *(cont.)*

2 x 0 =	
2 x 1 =	
2 x 2 =	
2 x 3 =	
2 x 4 =	
2 x 5 =	
2 x 6 =	
2 x 7 =	
2 x 8 =	
2 x 9 =	

3 x 0 =	
3 x 1 =	
3 x 2 =	
3 x 3 =	
3 x 4 =	
3 x 5 =	
3 x 6 =	
3 x 7 =	
3 x 8 =	
3 x 9 =	

Multiplication Fact Forms *(cont.)*

4 x 0 =	
4 x 1 =	
4 x 2 =	
4 x 3 =	
4 x 4 =	
4 x 5 =	
4 x 6 =	
4 x 7 =	
4 x 8 =	
4 x 9 =	

5 x 0 =	
5 x 1 =	
5 x 2 =	
5 x 3 =	
5 x 4 =	
5 x 5 =	
5 x 6 =	
5 x 7 =	
5 x 8 =	
5 x 9 =	

Multiplication Fact Forms *(cont.)*

6 x 0 = ☐	7 x 0 = ☐
6 x 1 = ☐	7 x 1 = ☐
6 x 2 = ☐	7 x 2 = ☐
6 x 3 = ☐	7 x 3 = ☐
6 x 4 = ☐	7 x 4 = ☐
6 x 5 = ☐	7 x 5 = ☐
6 x 6 = ☐	7 x 6 = ☐
6 x 7 = ☐	7 x 7 = ☐
6 x 8 = ☐	7 x 8 = ☐
6 x 9 = ☐	7 x 9 = ☐

Multiplication Fact Forms *(cont.)*

8 x 0 =	
8 x 1 =	
8 x 2 =	
8 x 3 =	
8 x 4 =	
8 x 5 =	
8 x 6 =	
8 x 7 =	
8 x 8 =	
8 x 9 =	

9 x 0 =	
9 x 1 =	
9 x 2 =	
9 x 3 =	
9 x 4 =	
9 x 5 =	
9 x 6 =	
9 x 7 =	
9 x 8 =	
9 x 9 =	

Ordering Factors

This bag activity contains all the materials you need to teach the ordering or commutative property of multiplication and so much more. Through the process, students will learn to work together and talk about their choices. They will learn strategies to break down numbers in order to find their factors. Additionally, students will learn proper terminology for multiplication.

Materials and Preparation

➤ 1 large gift bag, labeled Ordering Factors

➤ 1 copy each of Ordering Factors–Step 1, 2, and 3 for each student, pages 33–35

➤ 1 copy of Ordering Factors Number Cards for each student, page 36. Put both sets in a plastic snack bag.

➤ 1 copy of Teaching Sheet for each student, page 37

➤ 1 small resealable plastic snack bag for each student

➤ scissors

Procedure

1. Use the Teaching Sheet to discuss the given terms with students.

2. Begin with the first sheet, Ordering Factors–Step 1. Have students use Number Cards on the Ordering Factors Sheets–Steps 1 and 2 by placing them in the boxes to make equations. They are intended to be more of a work board, to facilitate moving cards upon them as well as discussing the combinations taking place.

3. Work up to doing independent equations with changing the order of factors as your goal, Step 3. Give students a number to work with that has many factors. For example, for the product 12, students should come up with the following on their sheet: 2 x 6 = 12, 6 x 2 = 12, 3 x 4 = 12, 4 x 3 = 12, 3 x 2 x 2 = 12, 2 x 2 x 3 = 12.

4. Repeat the same steps switching the product each time.

Bag Tag ✂

Ordering Factors-Step 1

Let's think about making equations! Use your set of Number Cards (one card per box) to make combinations of factors that equal the given product. Once you have a combination, change the order and repeat the fact.

Product of

Choose two factors that equal the above product.

 **X** 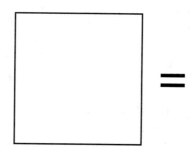 **=**

Now reorder the above combination.

 **X** 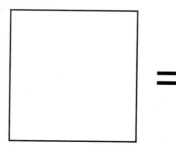 **=**

Well done! Write your equations for both.

___ **X** ___ **=** ___

___ **X** ___ **=** ___

Ordering Factors-Step 2

Let's think about making equations! Use your set of Number Cards (one card per box) to make combinations of factors that equal the given product. Once you have a combination, change the order and repeat the fact.

Product of

Choose three factors that equal the above product.

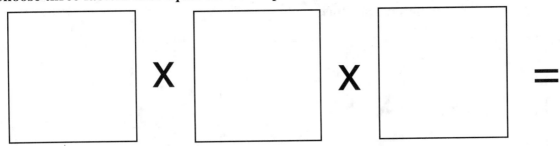

Now reorder the above combination.

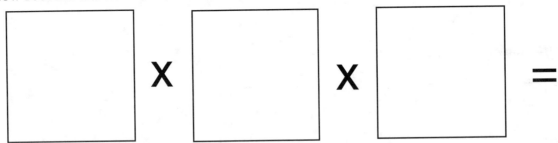

Now reorder the above combination again.

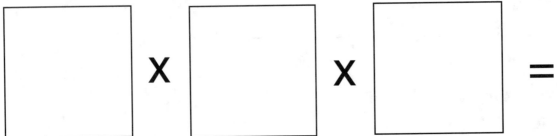

Well done! Write your equations for all three.

____ X ____ X ____ = ____

____ X ____ X ____ = ____

____ X ____ X ____ = ____

34   ©*Teacher Created Resources, Inc.*

Ordering Factors-Step 3

Let's make equations! With your partner or group, make as many equations as you can with the Number Cards to fit the given product. Remember to write the multiplication and equal signs where appropriate and show the use of the property of ordering factors.

Product of

Ordering Factors Number Cards

Copy and cut apart. Place in the boxes on pages 33 and 34 to make equations.

1	2	3	4	5
6	7	8	9	10

Here is a blank set of cards for you to write in your own numbers.

36

Teaching Sheet

The following are terms which you will need to know.

Equation: This is a written expression to show that two quantities are equal. It is the formal name for a number sentence. The quantities on both sides of the equal sign have the same value.

- Example: 3 x 4 = 12

- Three times four equals twelve.

- 3 x 4 has the same value as 12.

Factor: One of two or more numbers that when multiplied together produce a product.

- Example: 3 x 4 = 12

- The factors of 12 are 3 and 4.

Product: The result of multiplying two or more numbers (factors) together.

- Example: 3 x 4 = 12

- The product is 12.

Ordering Property of Multiplication: Another way to refer to the commutative property of multiplication. This rule says that changing the order of the factors will not change the product.

- Example: 3 x 4 = 12 and 4 x 3 = 12

- The placement of the 3 and the 4 on the left side of the equal sign does not change the product. They both produce a product of 12.

Place Value Mystery

With this bag activity, you will motivate students to think of strategies, use reasoning, and work collaboratively. It is a great problem-solving activity.

Materials and Preparation

➤ 1 medium gift bag, labeled Place Value Mystery

➤ 5 copies of Task Card and Number Tags, page 39, one per group

➤ 5 copies of Mystery Numbers, one of each per group, pages 40–41. Make one transparency of each for you.

➤ 5 resealable plastic snack bags to store Number Cards, one per group

➤ scissors

Procedure

1. Divide students into five groups. Give each group a Task Card, page 39. Read it with them, making any clarifications clear.

2. Next, have students cut apart the Number Tags, page 39.

3. Hand each group the copies of Mystery Numbers, while you have the same transparency on the overhead projector.

4. Read each problem out loud to the class, then allow time for students to work together to find a solution.

5. Encourage students to express their thinking and reasoning to their peers.

6. Call for groups to share their solutions, and then have students demonstrate how they found the solutions on the board or overhead, explaining as they share.

7. When they are finished, share the answers, and encourage students to share any methods that helped them come to their solutions.

Answers to Mystery Numbers (pages 40–41):

1. 8,642
2. 40,000
3. 999
4. 50

Extension: Upon completing the Place Value Mystery lesson, have each group create its own mystery numbers (up to four digits each) using the Blank Number Tags on page 39. Remind students to give a few clues, as the mystery numbers do in the lesson.

Bag Tag

Place Value Mystery

Task Card and Number Tags

Task

Carefully cut your numbers apart. With your group, you will need to solve the mystery numbers by using the clues given. As you decide, place the numbers on your work mats. All numbers will be used. Remember to discuss your reasoning for number choices with your group members.

Number Tags

5	8	0	0	2	9	0
4	9	0	4	6	0	9

Blank Number Tags

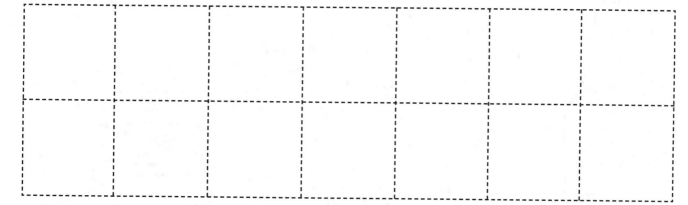

Mystery Numbers

1. This mystery number has four digits. Every digit is an even number. There are no repeating digits. There is an 8 in the thousands place. Each of the next three digits in this order, hundreds, tens, ones, is smaller than the one before it. What is the mystery number?

2. This mystery number has five digits. There is a 4 in the ten thousands place. None of the other digits is a 4. What is the smallest number that this mystery number could be?

Mystery Numbers *(cont.)*

3. This mystery number has three digits. All of the digits are the same. They are odd numbers. If you add 1 to the mystery number, you will get 1,000. What is the mystery number?

4. This mystery number has two digits. You will count it if you are counting by 5's to 100. It has a 0 in the ones place. It is half of 100. What is the mystery number?

Probability Matrix

With this matrix activity, students will gain insight and spend time learning how to look at statistics, variables, and collected data. It's a wonderful catalyst for encouraging extended thinking!

Materials and Preparation

➤ 1 medium gift bag, labeled Probability Matrix

➤ 5 copies of the Matrix Form for each student or group, page 43. You may also wish to have a transparency of this.

➤ 5 copies of the Matrix Form Worksheet for each student or group, page 44

➤ Suggested objects to toss, roll, or gather for data and then hypothesize probability:

- Large paper cups: toss to see how they land (on rim, bottom, or side)

- Checkers: toss to see how they land (star side or crown side)

- Dice: roll to see the number of times each number comes up

- Observe student posture during an assembly: Which posture can you guess you might see most often?

- Gather statistics on student lunches purchased: Which lunches are most likely to sell in the future?

Procedure

1. This lesson is to take place after an explanation about probability has been done. Begin a brainstorming session with the list of suggested ideas above. Have students generate several more ideas.

2. Tell students to choose five topics that they would like to test (individually or as a group). These topics should then be listed as the title, one per Matrix Form.

3. As an example, begin with the paper cups. Students can title it "Paper Cup Toss." For attributes, write *lands on bottom*, *lands on side*, and *lands on rim*.

4. Proceed by having 10 students toss the cup and record the results of each toss. Discuss the recorded results.

5. Have students draw conclusions by working through the four statements/questions on the Matrix Form Worksheet.

6. Students can do the activities in groups, testing a new topic each time.

Bag Tag ✂

Matrix Form

Title _____

Attributes ➔

Observations

⬇

1					
2					
3					
4					
5					
6					
7					
8					
9					
10					

Matrix Form Worksheet

1. Describe what you observed.

_____

_____

_____

_____

2. Explain the results.

_____

_____

_____

_____

3. What can you conclude from this?

_____

_____

_____

_____

4. Develop a hypothesis using the data you collected.

_____

_____

_____

_____

Problem Solving

Problem solving is a must! Students need to know it and they need to use it. They will use this skill for the rest of their lives. Teach them the basic strategies and let them know that assessment is ongoing (not only in math but in life as well) and your students will be successful. This bag activity contains the "how" with one activity. Be on the look out for other good problem-solving activities and tasks to add to this bag to increase your students' problem-solving skills. Keep a file in this bag until you have at least one challenging activity per week.

Materials and Preparation

➢ 1 medium gift bag, labeled Problem Solving

➢ 1 copy of Elsie's Garden per group, page 46

➢ 1 set of basic plastic pattern blocks per group (shapes needed: hexagons, triangles, trapezoids, rhombuses), or several copies of Pattern Blocks, page 47, cut apart

➢ 1 copy of the Assessment Checklist per group, page 48

➢ 1 copy of Problem Solving Strategies for each student, page 49. Optional: Enlarge this sheet to make it a classroom poster.

Procedure

1. Review the Problem Solving Strategies sheet with the class. Have students give examples to make sure they understand.

2. Go over the Assessment Checklist so students understand the expectations.

3. Create groups of four students and hand out Elsie's Garden task sheet to each group. Discuss it, and then distribute the pattern blocks to the students. Review the many uses of pattern blocks.

4. Allow groups to work together to solve Elsie's "problem."

5. Once all groups have found a solution and completed Elsie's Garden task sheet, have a class discussion and share the findings.

Bag Tag

Elsie's Garden

Can you help Elsie out? She needs to beautify her yard. Her garden must be made up of four different types of flowers. Also, she needs to do it on a low budget. She wants a very standard garden. She must complete her garden using the least expensive plants. Your task is to use pattern blocks of flowers to fill in this triangular plot at the cheapest price.

1. How many of each shape did you use for Elsie's Garden?

   _____

   _____

2. Show your design by tracing the outlines of the shapes directly onto the triangular space. What is the total cost of the garden?

   _____

3. Explain your decisions.

   _____

   _____

   _____

   _____

Pattern Blocks

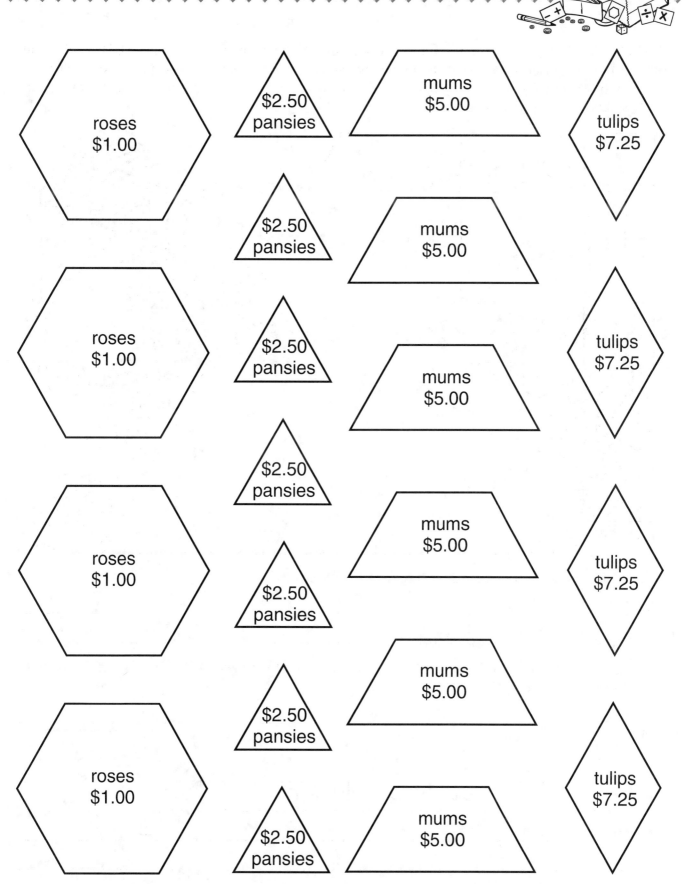

roses
$1.00

$2.50
pansies

mums
$5.00

tulips
$7.25

$2.50
pansies

roses
$1.00

$2.50
pansies

mums
$5.00

tulips
$7.25

mums
$5.00

$2.50
pansies

roses
$1.00

$2.50
pansies

mums
$5.00

tulips
$7.25

$2.50
pansies

mums
$5.00

roses
$1.00

$2.50
pansies

mums
$5.00

tulips
$7.25

Assessment Checklist

With your group, discuss and mark this checklist.

☐ Did we show our work?

☐ Did we restate the problem?

☐ Did we apply strategies?

☐ Did we explain our data?

☐ Did we state a solution?

Problem Solving Strategies

Act it Out 	Draw a Picture 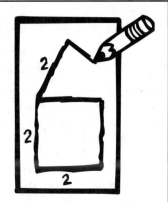
Make a Table	Use Logical Reasoning 
Look for Patterns 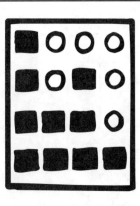	Guess and Check 
Make a List 	Brainstorm to get New Ideas 

Regrouping Work Mats

This activity uses base ten blocks (thousand cubes, hundred squares, tens rods, and ones cubes) in a very visual way to help students understand the concept of regrouping numbers to add and subtract.

Materials and Preparation

➤ 1 medium gift bag, labeled Regrouping Work Mats

➤ Several copies of the Regrouping Work Mats for addition and subtraction, pages 51–52

➤ a class set of wood or plastic base ten blocks (thousands, hundreds, tens, and ones), or paper Base Ten Blocks, page 53, copy and cut apart

Procedure

1. Give students an Addition or Subtraction Regrouping Work Mat. They will write numbers to add or subtract on the given lines, either by dictation, choice, roll of dice, etc.

2. Before adding or subtracting, they need to lay the number out visually with the base ten blocks in the appropriate boxes on their paper. Optional: Due to the space constraints, it is recommended that you give students blank sheets of 8.5" x 11" paper as needed and label them *ones*, *tens*, *hundreds*, and *thousands*. This will allow for students to have a much larger Work Mat similar to the one provided.

3. They should show you the process by manipulating the pieces to display their answers. See example to the right.

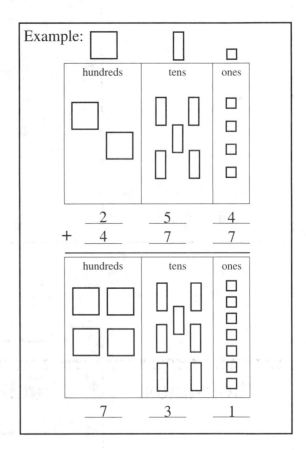

Bag Tag

Addition Regrouping Work Mat

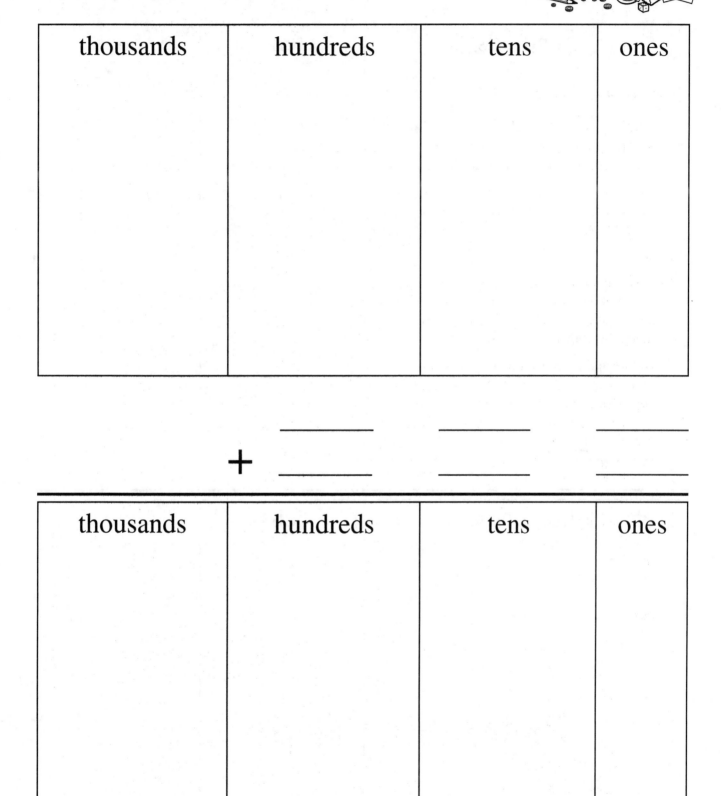

thousands	hundreds	tens	ones

$+$ ____ ____ ____

thousands	hundreds	tens	ones

Subtraction Regrouping Work Mat

hundreds	tens	ones

— _____ _____ _____

hundreds	tens	ones

Base Ten Block Patterns

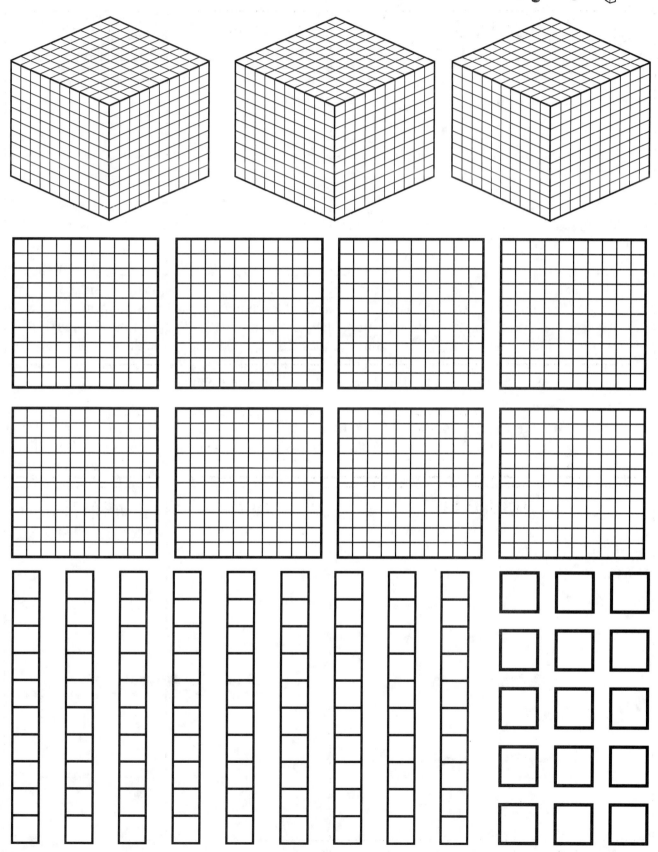

Rounding, Up or Same?

In this flashcard activity for rounding, you are going to keep the focus narrow. You will cue the student to the numbers that make the difference . . . the numbers that count in rounding. In oral drills, students need only respond with the word *up* or the word *same*. The rounding activity is easy, yet structured, and makes for a wonderful transfer of the skill.

Materials and Preparation

➤ 1 small gift bag, labeled Rounding, Up or Same?

➤ 1 set of Rounding Flashcards cut apart, pages 55–60. (You may choose to use heavy cardstock and laminate if possible.)

Procedure

1. You may wish to separate cards by nearest ten, hundred, or thousand at first. This lesson works best as a small group activity.

2. Show the flashcards to students one at a time. Ask them to tell you if the boxed digit or digits tells that they should round the unboxed number up to the next higher number, or if it should stay the same. Their answer will be based on the standard teaching of rounding, which should precede this exercise. Make sure students understand the concept of the "5, 50, 500" rule. That is, if a two-digit number has a 5 or higher in the ones place, they round the digit in the tens place up. If it has a 4 or less in the ones place, the number in the tens place stays the same and the remaining number(s) becomes a zero. It holds true for three-digit numbers ending with 50, and four-digit numbers ending with 500.

   Examples: If a flashcard of number 85 is shown with the 5 boxed, the student should say, "The 5 tells me that 85 rounds up to 90." They should state their reasoning, then the answer. Or, with a flashcard for the number 835 with the 35 boxed, "The 35 is less than 50, so the 8 stays the same, and 835 rounds to 800."

3. Practice daily, making sure that all students get a chance at working with the different cards. In written work, students who need a visual might need to draw an arrow up. This will show you their thinking.

Bag Tag

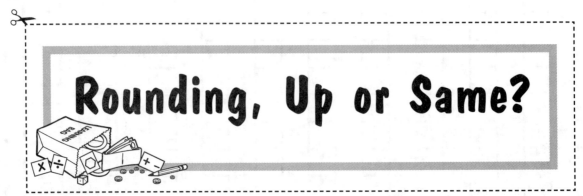

Rounding, Up or Same?

Nearest Ten Flashcards

7 8   2 7

4 2   9 1

5 1   3 3

6 7   4 5

Nearest Ten Flashcards *(cont.)*

6 2   2 1

4 6   8 3

8 8   3 7

6 5   5 8

Nearest Hundred Flashcards

4 21	1 75
2 43	9 10
5 64	3 39
6 71	4 50

Nearest Hundred Flashcards *(cont.)*

3 93

7 15

2 43

8 26

4 67

1 22

5 84

7 69

Nearest Thousand Flashcards

1,361	5,666
4,143	9,325
2,744	3,217
6,755	3,500

Nearest Thousand Flashcards *(cont.)*

7,568	5,265
4,224	9,415
2,474	3,702
6,853	3,885

Shopping Bag

With this bag activity, you will have the things necessary to create a simulated store activity.

Materials and Preparation

➤ 1–2 large gift bags (will hold all shopping items), labeled Shopping Bag; Bag Tag on page 62

➤ Several copies of Job Cards, page 62

➤ Several copies of Store Receipts, page 63

➤ Several copies of Customer Money, one for each customer, page 64. Copy the twenty-dollar bill onto green paper if possible.

➤ 1 flat plastic divided container that will serve as a cash register

➤ Assorted play money to make change

➤ About 40 items, tagged with prices (things around the room are great: chalk, crayons, pencils, books, rulers, etc.)

➤ 1 or 2 calculators

➤ tape

➤ stapler

➤ scissors

Procedure

1. Discuss and brainstorm with students how a real store operates. Be sure to discuss sales tax and what type of items are or are not taxed.

2. Explain that you would like the class to create a store. Determine the amount of sales tax and which items will or will not be taxed. Have students think about what they need to do in order for their class store to work. Have volunteers share their opinions.

3. Take all items from the bag (Price tags should already be attached.) and have students think of a way to organize. Ask students to think about how many clerks they might need? How many students should be customers? Workers? Managers? Select students for each type of position. Then distribute Job Cards and ask students to tape them to their shirts.

4. Encourage the managers and workers to set up a table of items.

5. Customers will get a Paper Wallet filled with money ($20). They will also get a Store Receipt. Customers need not collect any items while shopping; they are just to write what they would like to purchase and how many of each they would like. Remind students that they can only spend up to twenty dollars total, including tax.

6. You (teacher) should work side-by-side with the managers, suggesting things that will work. Managers may even need to hire an additional clerk if the line gets too long!

7. Using calculators, clerks or workers should add up totals including tax, count money, and make change. Make it as "real-life" as possible.

8. When shopping is over, be sure to talk about everyone's experiences.

Shopping Bag *(cont.)*

Bag Tag

Job Cards

Customer	Clerk
Manager	Worker

Store Receipts

Classroom Store

Quantity	Description	Price Each	Total
		Subtotal	
		Tax	
		Total Purchase	

Classroom Store

Quantity	Description	Price Each	Total
		Subtotal	
		Tax	
		Total Purchase	

Customer Money

Paper Wallet

Copy, cut along solid line, fold lengthwise on dashed line, and staple on sides. Fill with a twenty-dollar bill from below. Have students personalize their wallets by creating a design and writing their names.

Name _____

Twenty-Dollar Bill